How to Analyze the Films of

QUENTIN
TARANTINO

by Mary K. Pratt

ABDO
Publishing Company

Essential Critiques

How to Analyze the Films of

QUENTIN TARANTINO

by Mary K. Pratt

Content Consultant: Michele Schreiber, PhD
assistant professor, Department of Film Studies, Emory University

Credits

Published by ABDO Publishing Company, 8000 West 78th Street, Edina, Minnesota 55439. Copyright © 2011 by Abdo Consulting Group, Inc. International copyrights reserved in all countries. No part of this book may be reproduced in any form without written permission from the publisher. The Essential Library™ is a trademark and logo of ABDO Publishing Company.

Printed in the United States of America,
North Mankato, Minnesota
062010
092010

 THIS BOOK CONTAINS AT LEAST 10% RECYCLED MATERIALS.

Editor: Mari Kesselring
Copy Editor: Jennifer Joline Anderson
Interior Design and Production: Marie Tupy
Cover Design: Marie Tupy

Library of Congress Cataloging-in-Publication Data
Pratt, Mary K.
  How to analyze the films of Quentin Tarantino / Mary K. Pratt.
      p. cm. — (Essential critiques)
  Includes bibliographical references.
  ISBN 978-1-61613-529-4
  1. Tarantino, Quentin—Criticism and interpretation—Juvenile literature. I. Title.
  PN1998.3.T358P73 2010
  791.4302'33092—dc22

                                  2010007477

Table of Contents

Chapter

1

Introduction to Critiques

What Is Critical Theory?

What do you usually do as a member of an audience during a movie? You probably enjoy the settings, the costumes, and the sound track. You learn about the characters as they are developed through dialogue and other interactions. You might be drawn in by the plot of the movie, eager to find out what happens next. Yet these are only a few of many ways of understanding and appreciating a movie. What if you are interested in delving more deeply? You might want to learn more about the director and how his or her personal background is reflected in the film. Or you might want to examine what the film says about society—how it depicts the roles of women and minorities, for example. If so, you have entered the realm of critical theory.

Critical theory helps you learn how various works of art, literature, music, theater, film, and other endeavors either support or challenge the way society behaves. Critical theory is the evaluation and interpretation of a work using different philosophies, or schools of thought. Critical theory can be used to understand all types of cultural productions.

There are many different critical theories. If you are analyzing a movie, each theory asks you to look at the work from a different perspective. Some theories address social issues, while others focus on the director's life or the time period in which the movie was written or set. For example, the critical theory that asks how a director's life and filmmaking style affected the work is called auteur criticism. Other common, broad schools of criticism include historical criticism, feminist criticism, and ideological criticism. New Criticism examines a work solely within the context of the work itself.

What Is the Purpose of Critical Theory?

Critical theory can open your mind to new ways of thinking. It can help you evaluate a movie from a new perspective, directing your attention to issues and messages you may not otherwise recognize in a work. For example, applying feminist criticism to film may make you aware of female stereotypes perpetuated in the work. Applying a critical theory to a work helps you learn about the person who created it or the society that enjoyed it. You can explore how the movie is perceived by current cultures.

How Do You Apply Critical Theory?

You conduct a critique when you use a critical theory to examine and question a work. The theory you choose is a lens through which you can view the work, or a springboard for asking questions about the work. Applying a critical theory helps you to think critically about the work. You are free to question the work and make an assertion about it. If you choose to examine a movie using auteur theory, for example, you want to know how the director's personal background, education, or filmmaking techniques inspired or shaped the work. You could explore why the director wanted to tell this story in this way. For instance, are there any parallels between a particular character's life and the director's life?

Forming a Thesis

Ask your question and find answers in the work or other related materials. Then you can create a thesis. The thesis is the key point in your critique. It is your argument about the work based on the tenets, or beliefs, of the theory you are using. For example, if you are using biographical theory to ask how the director's life inspired the work, your thesis could be worded as follows: Director Teng Xiong, raised in refugee camps in southeast Asia, drew upon her experiences in writing and directing the film *No Home for Me*.

> ### How to Make a Thesis Statement
>
> In a critique, a thesis statement typically appears at the end of the introductory paragraph. It is usually only one sentence long and states the author's main idea.

Providing Evidence

Once you have formed a thesis, you must provide evidence to support it. Evidence might take the form of examples and quotations from the work itself, such as dialogue from a movie. Articles about the film or personal interviews with the director might also support your ideas. You may wish to address what other critics have written about the work. Quotes from these individuals may help support your claim. If you find any quotes or examples that contradict your thesis, you will need to create an argument against them. For instance, Many critics have pointed to the heroine of *No Home for Me* as a powerless victim of circumstances. However, at the end of the film, she is clearly depicted as someone who seeks to shape her own future.

> ### How to Support a Thesis Statement
>
> A critique should include several arguments. Arguments support a thesis claim. An argument is one or two sentences long and is supported by evidence from the work being discussed.
>
> Organize the arguments into paragraphs. These paragraphs make up the body of the critique.

In This Book

In this book, you will read overviews of movies directed by Quentin Tarantino, each followed by a critique. Each critique will use one theory and apply it to one work. Thinking Critically sections will give you a chance to consider other theses and questions about the work. Did you agree with the author's application of the theory? What other questions are raised by the thesis and its arguments? You can also find out what other critics think about each particular film. Then, in the You Critique It section in the final pages of this book, you will have an opportunity to create your own critique.

Look for the Guides

Throughout the chapters that analyze the works, thesis statements have been highlighted. The box next to the thesis helps explain what questions are being raised about the work. Supporting arguments have been underlined. The boxes next to the arguments help explain how these points support the thesis. Look for these guides throughout each critique.

Quentin Tarantino

2

A Closer Look at Quentin Tarantino

In true Hollywood fashion, Quentin Tarantino burst onto the moviemaking scene with *Reservoir Dogs*, his 1992 crime drama. He became an overnight sensation, seemingly coming out of nowhere to win critical acclaim with this complex and brutal tale of a robbery gone wrong. But in reality, Tarantino had been working for years toward his goal of becoming a filmmaker.

Quentin Tarantino was born on March 27, 1963, in Knoxville, Tennessee. His parents had separated before his birth, and Quentin was raised by his mother. Quentin and his mother moved to Los Angeles, California, when he was two years old. Movies were a part of Quentin's life from an early age. He and his mother often took trips to the movie theater. But Quentin was not seeing the usual

G-rated films other children his age enjoyed. From the time he was six years old, his mother took him to see adult movies.

A Gifted Child

Although extremely intelligent, Quentin did not do well in school. His teachers thought he was too hyperactive. When Quentin was 16 years old, his mother allowed him to drop out of school, but she told him he would need to find a job. Quentin found work as an usher in a theater that showed pornographic movies.

Despite his academic problems, Quentin had high ambitions. He wanted to be an actor. "I've known what I was trying to do since I was in first grade, that I wanted to be an actor, and so that's why I quit school, to start studying acting," Quentin said.[1]

Learning His Craft

Tarantino took acting classes for more than five years. In 1983, when he was 20, he started working at a video store called Video Archives. The job gave him free access to as many videos as he liked. This fed Tarantino's appetite for movies and filmmaking.

Quentin Tarantino has always had an off-beat approach to life.

Tarantino worked to hone his screenwriting skills during this time, cowriting, directing, and acting in his own short film, *My Best Friend's Birthday*. He also wrote the scripts for *Natural Born Killers* and *True Romance*. Other scripts followed, including *Reservoir Dogs*. Meanwhile, Tarantino continued to pursue acting roles, appearing as an Elvis impersonator in an episode of the television series *The Golden Girls*. However, it was as a writer and filmmaker, and not as an actor, that he would become known.

Tarantino's first major film, *Reservoir Dogs*, debuted at the Sundance Film Festival on January 18, 1992. A review that appeared in the *New York Times* called *Reservoir Dogs* "one of the most aggressively brutal movies," but also noted its "dazzling cinematic pyrotechnics and over-the-top dramatic energy" as well as the "breathtaking effect" of its complex structure.[2]

Earning Critical Praise

Tarantino followed his critically acclaimed debut film with *Pulp Fiction* in 1994, which he had written with Video Archives co-worker Roger Avary. *Pulp Fiction* was awarded the Palme d'Or, the highest prize at the Cannes Film Festival. It was nominated for seven Academy Awards, winning an Oscar for Best Original Screenplay.

The movie *Natural Born Killers*, based on Tarantino's original story and directed by Oliver Stone, also came out in 1994, garnering Tarantino more attention and praise. "What he writes blows people away. . . . Critics and audiences have crowned him Hollywood's Next Big Thing," Tim Appelo wrote in the December 30, 1994, issue of *Entertainment Weekly*.[3]

Tarantino in 2009

With his early successes, Tarantino was well established as a film writer and director by the mid-1990s. Since then, his body of work has expanded to include *Jackie Brown* (1997), *Kill Bill: Volume 1* (2003), *Kill Bill: Volume 2* (2004), *Death Proof* (2007), and *Inglourious Basterds* (2009). Tarantino's reputation as an innovative filmmaker was cemented at the Sundance Film Festival in January 2008, when he was honored with a Ray-Ban Visionary Award for his passion, creativity, and originality.

A movie poster for *Reservoir Dogs*

Chapter

3

An Overview of
Reservoir Dogs

Tarantino's 1992 movie *Reservoir Dogs* is a film noir that tells the story of a jewelry store robbery gone wrong. Unlike most films, *Reservoir Dogs* does not follow a linear narrative that starts at a particular point in time and ends at a later point in time. Rather, the story jumps back and forth from present to past, gradually revealing information about the plot and the characters.

The movie opens with eight men sitting around a table in a diner. Nearly all of them are wearing dark suits with white shirts and narrow black ties. When the bill comes, the men discuss the practice of tipping. One man says he does not tip waitresses just because society expects him to. The others argue with him, some defending waitresses and a few adding sexual commentary. The opening credits come next, as the "reservoir dogs" are shown walking down the street. The "dogs," as will be revealed over the course of the story, are six criminals using the aliases of Mr. Blonde, Mr. Brown, Mr. White, Mr. Orange, Mr. Pink, and Mr. Blue, along with Joe Cabot and his son "Nice Guy" Eddie, who will be the leaders of a heist.

Who Is the "Rat"?

In the next scene, Mr. Orange is sprawled in the back of a speeding getaway car, bleeding all over the white leather interior. He screams that he is going to die and begs the driver, Mr. White, to take him to a hospital. Mr. White promises to get him a doctor once they make it to the rendezvous location.

The pair arrives at an empty warehouse. Mr. White, who gives his real name as Larry, drags the wounded Mr. Orange into the building. He comforts Mr. Orange, combs his hair, and wipes his brow with a white handkerchief. He tells him he will be okay once Joe arrives and arranges for a doctor.

Soon, Mr. Pink bursts into the warehouse. As Mr. Orange lies unconscious in another room, Mr. Pink and Mr. White run through what happened during the botched robbery. Their dialogue reveals that an alarm was triggered, and the police arrived much earlier than expected. Each man scrambled to escape, and Mr. Brown (played by Tarantino) was shot dead by the police. Amid the mayhem, Mr. Blonde shot and killed several people. Mr. Pink believes that one of their crew tipped off the police, and reminds Mr. White not to tell anyone his real name, as nobody can be trusted.

As Mr. Pink tells his story, the movie flashes back to show how he ran from police and hijacked a car in order to make his escape. Mr. Pink reveals that he has managed to get away with a bag of stolen diamonds. He has stashed them away, planning to wait until all the accomplices make it to the warehouse and can determine which one of crew is the rat, or police informant.

Mr. White confesses that he told Mr. Orange his real name in the getaway car. He did so in order to comfort the man, who appeared to be dying. Mr. Pink is rattled and angry; if Mr. Orange is a police informant, he could use Mr. White's real name in order to get information about the rest of the team. The argument between White and Pink escalates until they pull guns on each other.

Mr. Blonde

Just then another accomplice, Mr. Blonde, arrives. Mr. White blames Mr. Blonde for the fiasco, calling him a "trigger-happy madman."[1] Mr. Pink again declares that someone is a "rat."[2] Mr. Blonde remains calm, telling them that "Nice Guy" Eddie will be arriving soon to sort things out. He then leads the others outside to his car and shows them a police officer tied up in his trunk.

In a flashback, Mr. Blonde, also known as Vic Vega, is shown being recruited for the heist by Joe and "Nice Guy" Eddie. It is revealed that Vic had been jailed for a past crime involving Joe. However, Vic remained loyal to Joe and did not reveal any information to the police about this connection.

The movie cuts back to the warehouse. The men are beating the police officer to find out whether the incident was a setup, but the officer claims to know nothing. "Nice Guy" Eddie, who has since arrived, dismisses the idea of a setup. He tells the others Joe is on his way and he is angry about the mess. Eddie then takes Mr. Pink and Mr. White to hide the cars and retrieve the stolen diamonds.

Mr. Blonde is now alone in the warehouse with the tied-up police officer and the unconscious

Mr. Orange. He calmly admits he does not care to torture the officer for information, but will do so simply because "it's amusing to me to torture a cop."[3] In what is one of the movie's most famous as well as disturbing scenes, Mr. Blonde dances to the lighthearted 1970s song "Stuck in the Middle with You" by Stealer's Wheel while holding a razor. He slices off the officer's ear. Next, he gets a can of gasoline from his car, pours it on the helpless man, and readies his lighter to start him on fire.

Suddenly, Mr. Orange awakens and shoots Mr. Blonde dead. He reveals he is a police officer working undercover. The tied-up officer responds, "I know. Your name is Freddy."[4] He tells Mr. Orange the police are just a block away, waiting until Joe shows up before making a move.

The movie flashes back to the story of Mr. Orange. An undercover police officer, he was recruited by Joe for the jewelry store robbery. A new scene shows Joe instructing his crew on the planned robbery.

Another flashback reveals more about what happened immediately after the robbery and shows how Mr. Orange was injured. A wounded Mr. Brown is shown driving from the scene with Mr.

Orange and Mr. White in the car. Mr. Brown crashes the car and dies, leaving the other two to flee on foot. Mr. Orange and Mr. White hijack another vehicle. When the female driver pulls a gun and shoots Mr. Orange in the stomach, Mr. Orange shoots back, killing her.

A Bloody Finale

The action cuts back to the warehouse, where Mr. Orange and the tortured officer remain. Eddie, returning with Mr. Pink and Mr. White, is aghast to find Mr. Blonde dead and demands to know why he was killed. Mr. Orange lies that Mr. Blonde had gone crazy and planned to kill everyone so he could take the diamonds for himself. Eddie angrily shoots the tied-up officer dead. He does not buy Orange's story; Mr. Blonde was loyal while in jail and would not betray his criminal comrades now.

At last, Joe arrives and learns about what has happened. He suspects Mr. Orange as the rat, but Mr. White comes to Orange's defense, calling him a "good kid."[5] As the arguing escalates, Eddie, Joe, and Mr. White all draw their guns in a standoff. After a few tense moments, shots are fired. Joe and Eddie fall dead and Mr. White is badly wounded.

Mr. Pink sneaks out, taking the diamonds. Mr. White manages to crawl over to Mr. Orange, cradling him in his arms. Sirens wail outside, and Mr. Pink is heard being captured and shot by police. Orange, moved by White's affection and loyalty, confesses the truth: he was the rat all along. Mr. White, sobbing in despair, points the gun at Mr. Orange's head. Police swarm the room and tell Mr. White to drop the gun or they will shoot him. But Mr. White shoots Mr. Orange and simultaneously the police shoot Mr. White dead.

Violence is a common theme in *Reservoir Dogs*.

Mr. Blonde

4

How to Apply Gender Criticism to *Reservoir Dogs*

What Is Gender Criticism?

Gender criticism explores how ideas about gender roles are reflected in works of art and literature. Critics using this approach consider how male and female characters behave, how they interact, and how they are perceived. Although related to feminist criticism, which examines a piece through a feminist lens, gender criticism is broader in that it can analyze both masculine and feminine gender roles.

Applying Gender Criticism to *Reservoir Dogs*

Tarantino's big-screen debut, *Reservoir Dogs*, is more than just a crime drama. It is the story of manhood: what it takes to be a man and to be part of the fellowship of men. Author Jeff

Dawson called the movie a "tense macho drama."[1] Women are almost completely absent from the film, and when they are acknowledged, it is usually in derogatory terms. With its focus exclusively on a gang of male criminals and tough cops, *Reservoir Dogs* depicts a uniform sense of masculinity as violent, disrespectful of women, and contemptuous of "weak" feelings such as empathy and trust.

The men in the film are presented as similar to each other, creating a unified sense of manhood among them. The opening scene of *Reservoir Dogs*, which shows the eight men gathered in a diner, draws viewers into a macho world. The dialogue is peppered with obscenities and jibes. The six anonymous members of Joe's crew are dressed the same, in

---

Thesis Statement

In the first paragraph, the author presents the thesis: "With its focus exclusively on a gang of male criminals and tough cops, *Reservoir Dogs* depicts a uniform sense of masculinity as violent, disrespectful of women, and contemptuous of 'weak' feelings such as empathy and trust." This thesis addresses the question of how masculinity is depicted in the film.

Argument One

The author has started to argue the thesis. "The men in the film are presented as similar to each other, creating a unified sense of manhood among them." This point addresses the first part of the thesis, about how the men are grouped together in a similar idea of maleness. The author will back up this point with evidence from the movie.

dark suits with white shirts and dark ties—a sort of uniform. Already, men are the focus of the film. The women are waitresses who serve the men.

Mr. White, *right*, with the injured Mr. Orange

The uniform sense of manhood is reinforced by how the male characters are identified. Most of them are stripped of their own names, and thus their individual identities. Instead, they are known by their assigned code names with the decidedly male mister in front of each. Mr. Pink argues against his assigned name because it sounds too feminine.

But image and language are not the only factors that create a hyped-up version of maleness

Argument Two

The author has turned to the next point in the thesis, focusing on how the male characters are presented as "aggressors."

in *Reservoir Dogs*; <u>these male characters present the stereotype of men as aggressors.</u> Disagreements between the men escalate quickly to threats of violence. When Mr. White and Mr. Pink argue after the heist, they pull guns on each other. In the final scene, Mr. White, Joe, and Eddie draw guns in an impossible standoff. The men use violence as their first tool to deal with their problems in almost all cases.

Argument Three

In her next argument, the author focuses on how the men in the movie relate to women, asserting, "Masculinity in this film is further defined by a lack of respect for women."

<u>Masculinity in this film is further defined by a lack of respect for women.</u> The men's conversations about women are often sexually graphic and vulgar. For example, in the opening scene the men discuss their interpretation of Madonna's 1984 song, "Like a Virgin," using obscene terms. They joke about what a waitress should do sexually to earn a tip from Mr. Pink. The men do not see women as equals. Mr. Blue, for example, calls the waitress a girl even though she is an adult. In other scenes of the movie, women only appear as victims.

The men in
Reservoir Dogs
are aggressive.

One is dragged from her vehicle; another is shot
dead when attempting to defend herself from a
carjacking.

<u>The men in the film are</u>
<u>stripped of any characteristic</u>
<u>that would deem them "weak,"</u>
<u>or unaggressive. The male</u>
<u>characters, for the most part,</u>
<u>display little or no empathy and</u>
<u>are incapable of trust.</u> Consider,
for instance, that three of the
criminals end up in a standoff,
with guns pointed at each other in a circle of
mistrust that ensures their mutual deaths. In this

> **Argument Four**
> The author argues the final
> part of the thesis, presenting
> evidence to show that "The
> men in the film are stripped
> of any characteristic that
> would deem them 'weak,'
> or unaggressive. The male
> characters, for the most part,
> display little or no empathy
> and are incapable of trust."

criminal world, the one example of compassion occurs between Mr. White and undercover police officer Mr. Orange. When Mr. Orange is injured, Mr. White consoles him. At the end of the film in a gesture of kindness, Mr. White cradles Mr. Orange's head. Trusting Mr. White, Mr. Orange confesses that he is the rat. In response, Mr. White shoots him. Mr. Orange's moment of trust backfires, leading to his death. On the other side, Mr. White's empathy for Mr. Orange is a mark of weakness. He commits the error of trusting and caring for another man—and that leads to his downfall. The police kill him.

Conclusion

This final paragraph is the conclusion of the critique. It sums up the author's arguments and partially restates the original thesis, which has now been argued and supported with evidence.

There is no doubt the world depicted in *Reservoir Dogs* is not just a man's world but an exaggerated version of it. This movie's version of manhood is one in which empathy, forgiveness, and concern for life are out of place; violence reigns. Viewers of the film may be shocked and disgusted by this portrayal of a senselessly violent, dog-eat-dog world in which the "dogs" all kill each other off in the end.

Thinking Critically about *Reservoir Dogs*

Now it is your turn to assess the critique. Consider these questions:

1. What do you think of the author's thesis? Can you find other instances of stereotypically masculine behavior in the film? If so, what are they? How do they support the thesis?

2. What was the most interesting argument made? What was the strongest one? What was the weakest? Were the points backed up with strong evidence from the film? Did the arguments support the thesis?

3. What conclusion would you make about the film based on this author's argument? What message does the film seem to convey overall?

Other Approaches

What you have just read is one possible way to apply gender criticism to the film *Reservoir Dogs*. What are some other ways to apply this approach? Remember that gender criticism focuses on how gender is portrayed in a work. Following are two alternate approaches.

A Response to the "Crisis of Masculinity"

Some critics have claimed that *Reservoir Dogs* and other ultramacho films like it are responses to a modern "crisis of masculinity." According to this theory, men today feel threatened by the increased power and equality of women in society and, as a result, are drawn to portrayals of overtly aggressive, dominant masculinity as a form of fantasy.

The thesis statement for a critique that examines the film's relation to the crisis of masculinity might be: The ultramacho *Reservoir Dogs* is a response to the crisis of masculinity in American society, providing a cathartic fantasy world for the modern male viewer.

Same-Sex Desire

Many critics have pointed to scenes in *Reservoir Dogs* as homoerotic, or suggestive of sublimated homosexual desire. The scene in which Mr. White cradles the injured Mr. Orange is often cited as an example. Author Gary Indiana makes this claim, in part, when he states, "*Reservoir Dogs* is an all-male, all-macho, grindingly homoerotic film." [2]

The thesis statement for such a critique could be: The relationship between Mr. White and Mr. Orange in *Reservoir Dogs* is a thinly veiled representation of same-sex desire in a hypermacho world.

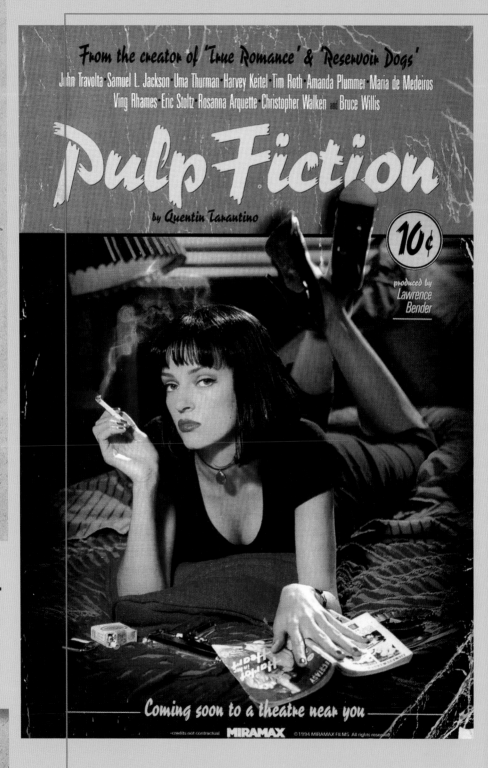

A movie poster for *Pulp Fiction*

An Overview of
Pulp Fiction

The 1994 film *Pulp Fiction* is made up of several
different stories. As the movie's first scene begins,
a man and a woman, calling each other Pumpkin
and Honey Bunny, are talking in a restaurant
booth. As the conversation continues, it is revealed
that the pair has a career robbing liquor stores.
Abruptly, they decide to try robbing the restaurant.
This affectionate, seemingly quiet couple pulls out
guns, waves them at the other diners, and begins
screaming out threats. The opening credits roll.

Jules and Vincent

The action cuts to a new scene. Two gangsters,
Jules and Vincent, are together in a car, with Jules
driving. Vincent, who has just returned from a
trip to Europe, informs Jules that a McDonald's

Quarter Pounder with cheese is called a "royale with cheese" in Paris. The mundane conversation continues and the two assassins pull out guns and head into a building. Among other things, they talk about their boss, Marsellus Wallace, and his wife, Mia. Marsellus has asked Vincent to take care of Mia while he is away in Florida. Jules warns Vincent of Marsellus's jealousy. Then, Vincent and Jules burst into an apartment and execute three men.

In the next scene, titled "Vincent Vega & Marsellus Wallace's Wife," a man named Butch is sitting in an empty restaurant with Marsellus Wallace. Marsellus gives Butch an envelope of cash, telling him, "In the fifth, your ass goes down."[1] Jules and Vincent, casually dressed in shorts, enter the restaurant to meet with Marsellus.

Vincent and Mia

That night, on his way to pick up Marsellus's wife, Mia, Vincent stops at the home of his drug dealer, Lance, to buy some heroin. Vincent is shown readying the heroin to inject and then driving his convertible. Then, Vincent arrives at the Wallaces' house to pick up Mia. Inside the house, Mia snorts lines of drugs, before going out to meet Vincent.

Vincent and Mia go to a 1950s-style restaurant. Seated in a booth, they talk about Mia's role on the pilot of a television show called *Fox Force Five*. Then, at Mia's insistence, they enter a dance contest.

Mia and Vincent perform in a dance contest.

Vincent and Mia return to the house. Vincent goes to the bathroom to collect himself. He tells himself the night was Marsellus's test of loyalty, and he is just going to say goodnight and leave.

Meanwhile, Mia finds Vincent's heroin, snorts it, and overdoses. Vincent finds her and panics.

Vincent drives Mia to Lance's house, where he convinces a reluctant Lance to help save Mia's life. Lance prepares an adrenaline shot and Vincent plunges it into Mia's heart, reviving her. Lance's wife, Jody, laughs and says, "That was . . . trippy!"[2] Vincent takes Mia home, and they agree never to tell Marsellus what happened.

Butch the Boxer

The movie then cuts to another story. Butch, a little boy, is watching a cartoon show on television. His mother introduces him to a man dressed in a military uniform. The soldier, Captain Koons, presents Butch with a gold wristwatch belonging to the boy's father, who died a prisoner of war in Vietnam. He explains that the watch had been in Butch's family for three generations.

The scene abruptly cuts to Butch as a grown man. Butch is waiting in his locker room for his boxing match to start. He wins the fight, killing his opponent, and flees the stadium in a taxi. Butch had made a deal with Marsellus to lose this fight.

Butch, who had bet heavily on himself, arrives at a hotel room, where he meets his girlfriend, Fabienne. They plan to run away together, but

Butch becomes enraged when he finds that his watch is missing from the luggage Fabienne packed for him. He tells her he has to return to his apartment to retrieve it.

Butch wins a boxing match he had promised to lose.

Butch drives back to his apartment, unaware Vincent is there waiting for him. Butch sneaks inside and finds the watch. Believing he is alone, he starts to make toaster pastries. Butch then spots a gun on the counter. He picks it up just as Vincent appears. Butch shoots Vincent dead.

Butch drives away. He stops at a red light. Just then, Marsellus walks by and recognizes Butch.

Butch rams the car into Marsellus and tries to flee, only to collide with another car. Marsellus and Butch start a chase on foot. They fight and stumble into a pawn shop. Butch punches out Marsellus. The shop owner pulls a gun and knocks out Butch.

Butch and Marsellus awaken to find themselves tied up in the basement of the pawn shop, where the shop owner and another man, Zed, intend to use them as sexual slaves. While the men sexually assault Marsellus, Butch breaks free and escapes. He hesitates at the door, and then goes back to rescue Marsellus, killing the owner. Marsellus grabs a gun and shoots Zed. Butch and Marsellus agree their dispute is over, but Marsellus tells Butch he must leave Los Angeles. Butch takes off on Zed's motorcycle, while Marsellus stays behind to wreak revenge on Zed.

Back to the Beginning

The movie flashes back to the scene in which Jules and Vincent execute the three men in the apartment. Jules quotes the Bible as he commits the execution. Another man bursts out of the bathroom with a gun and fires on the hit men, but somehow, all the bullets miss. Awestruck, Jules calls it "divine intervention."[3] Jules and Vincent kill the fourth man and then drive away from the murder scene, with an accomplice, Marvin, in the back seat. As Vincent turns toward the back to talk to Marvin, his gun goes off, killing Marvin. Jules and Vincent go to the home of Jules's friend Jimmy (played by Tarantino) and call Marsellus for help. Marsellus sends a man to organize the cleanup.

Jules and Vincent, who have traded their bloodstained dark suits for shorts and T-shirts, are getting breakfast at a diner and debating whether their escape from death was indeed a miracle from God. Vincent leaves for the bathroom just as Pumpkin and Honey Bunny start to rob the diner and its customers. Pumpkin demands the briefcase Jules is guarding, but Jules grabs hold of Pumpkin and aims his gun at him. A twitchy Honey Bunny points her gun at Jules and demands that he release Pumpkin. Vincent returns and aims his gun at Honey Bunny. Jules tells the robbers he is repenting his sins and will therefore spare their lives. He gets them to leave with what they have stolen, leaving his briefcase behind. Jules and Vincent exit the restaurant, tucking their guns into the waistbands of their shorts.

Tarantino on the set of *Pulp Fiction*

How to Apply New Criticism to
Pulp Fiction

What Is New Criticism?

New Criticism is a style of literary analysis
that first developed in the 1920s. It became more
established in 1941 with the publication of *The New
Criticism* by John Crowe Ransom. New Criticism
calls for a close reading, or detailed examination of
the work, including its structure, diction, imagery,
speech, and recurrent ideas and themes, with
the goal of determining how all these elements
combine to create a complex but unified work. It is
commonly applied to books, stories, and poetry.

Although usually applied to literature, New
Criticism may be applied to film because a film
starts as a written screenplay, which usually
includes action, dialogue, and setting. The entire
focus of New Criticism is on the work itself, which

Honey Bunny, *left,* and Pumpkin at the restaurant

is considered to stand on its own. No attention is given to the historical or cultural context or to the creator's personal life. Nothing outside of the work is important to the critique.

Applying New Criticism to *Pulp Fiction*

Pulp Fiction, the 1994 movie that won an Oscar for Best Original Screenplay, is a collection of intersecting stories sharing a common theme of moral ambiguity. The main characters in each story move from mundane discussions and everyday actions to acts of depravity and violence. But it is not just their transitions from the typical to the criminal that is striking—it is the ease with which they make these transitions. Through their actions and dialogue, the characters of *Pulp Fiction* present a world in which right and wrong, the civil and the criminal, are so intertwined that the characters seem unable to distinguish between good and bad.

This moral ambiguity is at play from the start of *Pulp Fiction*. The movie opens with a man and woman having breakfast at a diner. Although they seem like an average couple, their conversation reveals that they are armed robbers. The line between good and bad is further blurred when the affectionate pair, calling each other Pumpkin and Honey Bunny, decide to rob the restaurant right then and there, as though it were as normal as paying the bill at the end of their meal.

Thesis Statement

The thesis statement is presented in the first paragraph: "Through their actions and dialogue, the characters of *Pulp Fiction* present a world in which right and wrong, the civil and the criminal, are so intertwined that the characters seem unable to distinguish between good and bad." This thesis addresses what kind of society *Pulp Fiction* presents.

Argument One

The author has started to argue the thesis. "This moral ambiguity is at play from the start of *Pulp Fiction*." The author goes on to give examples of moral ambiguity from the beginning of the movie.

The juxtaposition of good and evil, comical and deadly serious, continues in the next scene. Assassins Jules and Vincent are driving to do a job, making small talk that ranges from the French name for a Quarter Pounder with cheese to whether foot massages can be considered sexual. Their friendly discussion seems wildly out of place, as the two assassins are on their way to commit murder for their boss, Marsellus. Once they arrive at their victims' apartment to perform the murders, Jules quotes the Bible as he shoots down his targets without any sense of irony.

The main characters are not the only ones who lack a moral compass. Indeed, nearly everyone in *Pulp Fiction* seems unable to express an appropriate sense of right and wrong. For example, when Mia is revived after a near-fatal drug overdose, one onlooker's response is to laugh and call the experience "trippy."[1] Consider, too, the moral ambiguity of Lance in this situation. He provides the drugs that nearly kill Mia, but he also provides the syringe of adrenaline to save her.

Argument Two

The author gives further examples of the moral ambiguity in the film, claiming: "Indeed, nearly everyone in *Pulp Fiction* seems unable to express an appropriate sense of right and wrong."

This intertwined sense of right and wrong also arises in the story of Butch, the boxer turned fugitive turned hero. He agrees to throw a fight, taking Marsellus's bribe to do so. But then he wins the fight, double-crossing Marsellus. Furthermore, Butch actually kills his opponent but shows no remorse for doing so. He callously blames the victim, saying his opponent would still be alive if he were a better fighter. But Butch does not seem completely coldhearted. He is loving and tender with his girlfriend. Even though he loses his temper when she forgets to pack his treasured watch, he is quick to apologize for not being clear with her about how much the watch means to him.

> **Argument Three**
> The author now focuses on a single main character in the movie, showing how the character's behavior supports the thesis: "This intertwined sense of right and wrong also arises in the story of Butch, the boxer turned fugitive turned hero."

The movie further plays with moral ambiguity when Butch returns to his apartment for his watch. Thinking he is safe, Butch stops to make toaster pastries. Yet he quickly turns from this innocent domestic act to cold-blooded murder when he shoots Vincent with Vincent's own gun. He later snickers at his triumph. Butch's moral seesawing is shown once again after he encounters Marsellus and both are tied up and targeted for assault. When Butch frees himself, he goes back to rescue his enemy, showing he is capable of pity and mercy even for those who are out to kill him.

Argument Four

In a fourth argument, the author focuses on a minor character to prove the thesis stretches across the entire film: "No character is immune to this teetering morality."

No character is immune to this teetering morality. Even Jimmy, one of the movie's secondary characters, jumps from everyday, mundane concerns to seriously depraved actions. Jules and Vincent show up at Jimmy's house looking for help hiding a dead body and cleaning up the car after a murder. Jimmy is not concerned about the dead man or the fact that he is involved in cleaning up a murder. Rather, he is concerned that his wife might come home early from work and get angry. When he is asked for linens to help clean up, Jimmy is reluctant to turn them over because they are the good linens he and his wife received as wedding presents.

Argument Five

The author continues the critique with a focus on the final scenes, noting: "The final scene of *Pulp Fiction* reinforces the dominant theme of moral ambiguity."

The final scene of *Pulp Fiction* reinforces the dominant

theme of moral ambiguity. Jules and Vincent walk into the restaurant Honey Bunny and Pumpkin are preparing to rob, thus bringing the movie full circle. Jules, convinced he has witnessed a miracle when the bullets missed him and Vincent, says he plans to repent for his sins. When the robbers demand his briefcase, he holds a gun on Pumpkin

The casual clothing of both Vincent, *left*, and Jules is put in juxtaposition to their violent acts.

but refrains from killing him. "I'm trying real hard to be the shepherd," Jules tells Pumpkin, convincing his would-be robbers to leave without a fight.[2] As Jules and Vincent leave the diner in their borrowed shorts and T-shirts—looking, as Jimmy put it, "like dorks" rather than hit men—Jules vows to retire from his work.[3] Yet his last act is to tuck his gun into his waistband, leaving it unclear whether he is ultimately redeemed from evil or will continue on as before.

Conclusion

This final paragraph is the conclusion of the critique. It sums up the author's arguments and partially restates the original thesis, which has now been argued and supported with evidence.

Thus, *Pulp Fiction* ends in the same place it starts, both literally and figuratively. It places an incredibly violent world in the midst of the typical. And in this world, characters do not display any sort of consistent morality. They move from ordinary acts to evil undertakings without hesitation or thought, demonstrating that in their lives the two are so interconnected that good and bad are truly indistinguishable.

Thinking Critically about *Pulp Fiction*

Now it is your turn to assess the critique. Consider these questions:

1. The author of this essay claims that *Pulp Fiction* presents a world in which there is no clear sense of right and wrong. Do you agree with this thesis? Why or why not?

2. Do you think the author made a strong argument? What were the strongest points? What were the weakest points? Can you think of any evidence the author could have added to this argument?

3. How is the society presented in *Pulp Fiction* different from or similar to the society we live in? Could a society such as this exist? What do you think?

Other Approaches

What you have just read is one possible way to apply New Criticism to a critique of *Pulp Fiction*. What are some other ways to apply the approach? Remember that New Criticism focuses solely on the work itself. Following are two alternate approaches.

The Theme of Redemption

In the essay "Shepherding the Weak: The Ethics of Redemption in Quentin Tarantino's *Pulp Fiction*," Todd F. Davis and Kenneth Womack focus not on the lack of morality in *Pulp Fiction*, but on the moral redemption of Jules and Butch. The essay concludes that "Tarantino establishes Jules as the moral center of his film, and [the film] takes on greater ethical force when Jules spares Pumpkin and Honey Bunny in the film's final moments."[4]

The thesis statement for a critique that focuses on the theme of redemption in *Pulp Fiction* might be: Although the film seems to portray a world with no morals, the mercy Jules and Butch show at the end of the film ultimately provides hope of moral redemption.

The Dialogue in *Pulp Fiction*

Many critics have pointed to the marriage of the quickly spoken dialogue in the film with its rapid action. In fact, the rapid dialogue and action seem to help push the film's plot forward.

The thesis statement for such a critique could be: The action and dialogue together propel the film's feverish plot.

PAM GRIER

is

Jackie
Brown

a Quentin Tarantino film

Jackie Brown, starring Pam Grier, debuted in 1997.

7

An Overview of
Jackie Brown

Tarantino's 1997 film, *Jackie Brown*, based on the 1992 novel *Rum Punch* by American writer Elmore Leonard, tells the story of a clever woman who makes the most of a dangerous situation. The title character, Jackie Brown, is a middle-aged black woman working as a flight attendant for a Mexican airline. To earn extra cash, she has been smuggling a gun dealer's money from Mexico into the United States.

After an opening sequence showing Jackie Brown in an airport, gun dealer Ordell Robbie is shown at home watching television. With him is his friend Louis Gara. Then, a man named Beaumont calls. He has been arrested for drunk driving and criminal possession of a pistol and needs Ordell's help. Ordell and Louis go to see bail bondsman

Max Cherry to get the $10,000 bond Beaumont needs.

In the next scene, Ordell visits Beaumont, who is now free on bail. Having provided the $10,000, he says he wants Beaumont's help on a job. Instead, Ordell drives to a vacant lot, where he shoots Beaumont dead. Ordell then calls Louis and shows him the body. Ordell explains that had he not killed Beaumont, Beaumont would have ratted him out to the police in exchange for a more lenient sentence.

Arrested

The next scene shows Jackie walking in a parking ramp at Los Angeles International Airport. She is stopped by a police detective, Mark Dargus, and an agent with the federal Bureau of Alcohol, Tobacco, and Firearms (ATF) named Ray Nicolette. They search her bags and find $50,000 in cash and some drugs. They ask her to help them get her boss, threatening her with the loss of her job and jail time. However, Jackie gives them no information about Ordell. Meanwhile, Ordell goes back to Max Cherry to arrange bond for Jackie.

When Max drops Jackie off at her apartment that evening, Ordell is waiting for her in his car.

Ordell and Jackie discuss the day's events. Ordell suspects Beaumont of having tipped off the investigators who conducted the search.

Ordell shuts off the lights and moves closer to Jackie, placing his hands around her neck. He asks, "You scared of me?"[1] Jackie responds by pulling a gun which she took from Max Cherry's car. She says she knows Ordell came to kill her to prevent her from ratting to the police, and that if he pays her at least $100,000, she will not turn him in. Ordell hesitates, saying that all his money is in Mexico.

A Plan

Jackie hatches a plan. She tells the two investigators she will cooperate with them in a sting and asks permission to leave the country and fly to Mexico so she can keep her job and help them get Ordell. Meanwhile, she tells Ordell that investigators are already on to him. To help him out, she will fly to Mexico and smuggle in the $500,000 he has stashed away in exchange for a payoff. Ordell agrees to give her 10 percent.

After talking to Ordell, Jackie sees Max. Without telling him the details of her plan, Jackie asks Max whether he would walk away with

$500,000 if given the chance. Max does not answer, but he does say he has been thinking about getting out of the bail bondsman business.

Moving Money

Next, Jackie does a trial run, moving just a small portion of Ordell's money out of Mexico and getting it to him via a female accomplice at a shopping mall while investigators supervise the exchange. Later, Jackie meets with Ray, the ATF agent, telling him Ordell is nervous and will only move $50,000 into the United States at this time. In fact, Jackie plans to bring in $500,000 more, but will only show investigators $50,000, while hiding the rest of the money deep in her bag. She arranges with Ordell to pass off the $500,000 to his girlfriend, Melanie, while, with Max's help, secretly planning to swindle Ordell as well.

In the bathroom on the airplane, Jackie puts her plan into motion. She hides most of the money in the bottom of her travel bag, putting an envelope with $50,000 on top. After she lands, Jackie meets with the federal agent, Ray, who counts the cash and marks the bills with ink. Jackie then goes into a fitting room at the mall, where she has arranged to

meet Melanie. Under the door of the fitting room, she passes Melanie a shopping bag containing the $50,000 in marked bills. She leaves the bulk of the cash behind in the dressing room for Max to retrieve.

Jackie and Max form a friendship and an alliance.

Jackie then rushes out into the mall, looking panicked and yelling for Ray. She tells him that Melanie burst in and stole the money; he believes her. Meanwhile, Louis and Melanie are walking through the parking lot looking for their van.

Melanie is getting on Louis's nerves. He shoots her, and then finds the van and leaves. Louis picks up Ordell and Ordell discovers that most of the money is missing and Melanie is dead. Louis tells Ordell he saw Max in the store where they exchanged the shopping bags. Ordell then shoots Louis.

Ordell calls Max, who lies that Jackie kept the money because she did not trust Melanie and wanted to make sure she got her 10 percent. Ordell goes with Max to Max's office to retrieve the cash from Jackie, but federal agent Ray Nicolette is there waiting to arrest him. As Ordell walks in, Jackie yells to Ray, "He's got a gun."[2] Ray shoots Ordell dead.

Three days later, Jackie says good-bye to Max at his office before leaving for Spain. She has left him with 10 percent of the cash as a fee for helping her out. They share a kiss, and Jackie drives away, listening to the song "Across 110th Street," with its story of doing what it takes to get by.

Max helps Jackie
successfully
swindle Ordell
and the police.

Jackie Brown works as a flight attendant.

How to Apply Historical Criticism to *Jackie Brown*

What Is Historical Criticism?

Historical criticism is one school of critical theory used to analyze a book, a film, a theater production, or a piece of art or music. A historical critique looks at the historical context in which a work was created. It determines how the work reflects the social, economic, and political realities of its time.

To apply a historical critique, an author must research the time period in which the work was created. He or she might find similarities between events of the time period and events occurring or discussed in the work itself. The critique can make conclusions about the work and how it is reflecting or dealing with issues occurring in the time it was created.

Mark, *left*, and Ray point out Jackie's social standing.

Applying Historical Criticism to *Jackie Brown*

Jackie Brown tells the story of a 44-year-old African-American woman working in a low-paying job as a flight attendant. To make extra cash, she smuggles money and drugs from Mexico for gun dealer Ordell Robbie. But when she is caught smuggling, she finds herself in a tight spot. A police detective and a federal agent pressure Jackie to cooperate with them and give them information on Ordell. If Jackie does not help them, they will send her to jail, and she will lose her job. Ordell, on the other hand, is prepared to kill Jackie to prevent her from ratting on him. Jackie does not seem to have many choices, but she knows she must look out for herself at all costs. Jackie represents the African-American underclass of the late twentieth century, particularly the women of this class, who when squeezed on all sides are forced to do what they must to get by.

The movie presents the idea early on that Jackie is a second-class citizen. When authorities find her with Ordell's money and drugs, they try to intimidate her by pointing out her lack of options in life. Jackie has been in legal trouble before, in 1985,

Thesis Statement
The thesis statement is in the first paragraph: "Jackie represents the African-American underclass of the late twentieth century, particularly the women of this class, who when squeezed on all sides are forced to do what they must to get by." This thesis addresses the question: How does *Jackie Brown* mirror the social and economic realities of the United States in the late twentieth century?

Argument One
The author has started to argue the thesis. "The movie presents the idea early on that Jackie is a second-class citizen." The author will back up this point in the rest of the paragraph with evidence from the movie.

when as a flight attendant for Delta she was arrested for smuggling drugs for a pilot. Jackie defends herself, saying they were her husband's drugs, and she got off. But police detective Mark Dargus points out the arrest, even 13 years later, has kept Jackie from getting a good job with the bigger airlines. As a result, she is left working with a second-rate airline. As Mark says, "You've been in the service industry nineteen years and all you make is $16,000 [a year] plus benefits. You didn't exactly set the world on fire, did you?"[1]

Mark continues, "If I was a 44-year-old black woman desperately clinging on to this one . . . little job I was fortunate enough to get, I don't think I'd think that I had a year to throw away [in jail]."[2]

The entire scene puts Jackie's position in society in perspective. Jackie is low on the societal totem pole, placed there by her criminal record and her age, gender, and race, and this greatly influences how she is treated and the opportunities she has in life. The working world will not allow her to move up to a better-

> **Argument Two**
>
> The author zeroes in on the factors that leave Jackie at a disadvantage: "Jackie is low on the societal totem pole, placed there by her criminal record and her age, gender, and race, and this greatly influences how she is treated and the opportunities she has in life."

paying job, and even the investigators see her as disposable.

Mark's comments reflect the prevailing institutional attitude toward the working poor, as represented by Jackie, in the 1990s. The working poor—people who had jobs but still could not make ends meet—did not earn enough to keep up with inflation. Government programs, such as job training and job-search assistance, declined as federal and state lawmakers cut funding. Higher-income males saw their incomes rise sharply in the last decades of the twentieth century. Even after all the social and political advances women made in the second half of the century, they still earned less than their male counterparts. African-American women fared even worse. Due to persistent discrimination, they were paid less than white and Asian-American women for the same work. They were more likely to live in poverty as well. Jackie's situation is not just about race, though. The late twentieth century saw a growing number of working poor from all ethnic groups.

> **Argument Three**
>
> In the third argument, the author ties *Jackie Brown* to the social realities of the 1990s: "Mark's comments reflect the prevailing institutional attitude toward the working poor, as represented by Jackie, in the 1990s."

Given that historical context, it is clearer why Jackie is motivated to make the choices she makes in the film. Jackie is not blind to her position. Talking to Max, she says she always feels like she is starting over, unable to ever get ahead. She says she has been waiting on people for 20 years with little to show for it. And she admits that if she goes to jail and loses her job, she will have to start all over again—and without much going for her, she will be stuck. Conveying just what that position in life means to her, she adds, "That shit is more scary than Ordell."[3]

> **Argument Four**
> The author argues the second part of the thesis: "Recognizing her status, Jackie is willing to do whatever she must to get herself out of her situation."

Recognizing her status, Jackie is willing to do whatever she must to get herself out of her situation. Unwilling to go to jail or agree to probation, Jackie forms a plan. She will set up Ordell, double-cross the police, and keep Ordell's money for herself. When she discusses her plan with Max, he tells her she is rationalizing her bad behavior. Jackie recognizes this, too. But, she responds, "That's what you do to go through with the shit you start, you rationalize."[4]

Jackie outsmarts both the authorities and her criminal boss, Ordell.

<u>Jackie lacks power, position, and money, but calls on her courage, resolve, and quick wit to help herself out of her situation.</u> Jackie finds her way out of her difficult situation, outsmarting both the authorities and the criminals who try to make her do their bidding and dirty work, but who have strongly underestimated her intelligence. Jackie exemplifies the idea that no matter how poor or disadvantaged a person is, success is possible with enough persistence.

Argument Five

The author further recognizes that Jackie is able to change her social status with the final point: "Jackie lacks power, position, and money, but calls on her courage, resolve, and quick wit to help herself out of her situation."

Conclusion

This final paragraph is the conclusion of the critique. It sums up the author's arguments and partially restates the original thesis, which has now been argued and supported with evidence. The author also challenges readers to consider the implications of the fact that Jackie Brown succeeds only through breaking the law and making questionable moral choices.

In the final scene, Jackie is seen driving away in Ordell's Mercedes, having pulled off a nearly half-million-dollar heist. She is mouthing the lyrics of the song "Across 110th Street": "Doing whatever I had to do to survive. I'm not saying what I did was alright; trying to break out of the ghetto was a day-to-day fight. Been down so long, getting up did not cross my mind, I knew there was a better way of life that I was just trying to find."[5] The song, sung by Bobby Womack, refers to African Americans living in Harlem, New York, but also seems to mirror the life of Jackie Brown. She takes great personal risk, makes moral compromises, and breaks the law—but in the end, it was all necessary for her own survival and success.

Thinking Critically about *Jackie Brown*

Now it is your turn to assess the critique. Consider these questions:

1. The thesis stresses that Jackie Brown is able to achieve a better life by taking big risks and being persistent. Do you think a person can achieve anything if he or she takes big risks and works persistently? What might prevent a person from reaching his or her goals?

2. Do you agree with the critique? What arguments did you agree with? What arguments did you find less convincing? Why?

3. This critique focuses on parallels between *Jackie Brown* and socioeconomic realities of the late twentieth century, but does this movie relate to the present time as well? What is the same? What is different?

Other Approaches

What you have just read is one possible way to apply historical criticism to the film *Jackie Brown*. What are some other ways to critique the film using historical criticism? Remember that historical criticism looks beyond what is in a movie; it examines what was happening in history during the time the movie was created and how that may have influenced the film. Following are two alternate approaches. The first puts more focus on race than the previous critique. The other examines the film as homage to 1970s pop culture.

The African-American Experience

Some critics have focused on the issue of race in *Jackie Brown*. As it features main characters who are African-American and multiple references to black culture, the film may be seen as a commentary on the African-American experience of the late twentieth century.

The thesis statement for such a historical critique might be: *Jackie Brown* reflects racial attitudes toward African Americans during the late twentieth century.

1970s Nostalgia

As many critics have noted, *Jackie Brown* pays homage to blaxploitation films of the 1970s. These films, targeted at an African-American audience, featured African-American actors, soul and funk music, and storylines involving hit men, drug dealers, and corrupt white officials. *Jackie Brown* has many of the same qualities as these films. The film may reflect a sense of 1970s nostalgia that sprung up in the 1990s, when pop culture from the 1970s was revived in many films and television shows.

The thesis statement for such a critique could be: The film *Jackie Brown* reflects a nostalgia for the 1970s that was prevalent in the last decade of the century.

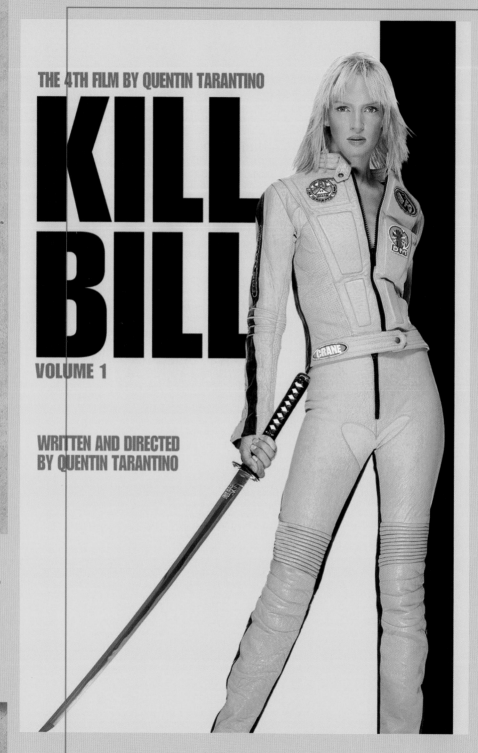

Kill Bill: Volume 1 was released in 2003. *Kill Bill: Volume 2* followed in 2004.

9

An Overview of
Kill Bill: Volume 1
and *Kill Bill: Volume 2*

Kill Bill: Volume 1 and *Kill Bill: Volume 2* are
two separate movies released in 2003 and 2004
respectively. They tell the story of one woman's
revenge on a villain named Bill. The woman,
known first as the Bride, and later by her real name
Beatrix Kiddo, is a trained assassin who worked for
Bill as a member of his Deadly Viper Assassination
Squad under the code name Black Mamba. After
discovering she is pregnant with Bill's child,
Beatrix leaves the team and plans to marry someone
else. However, Bill and his assassins show up at her
wedding rehearsal and massacre everyone there,
leaving Beatrix for dead. Waking up four years later
from a coma, Beatrix tracks down her assailants,
one by one, exacting bloody revenge as she seeks
out Bill.

Kill Bill: Volume 1 opens in black and white, showing the beaten and bloody face of Beatrix. She is lying on the floor. A man asks, "Do you find me sadistic?" as he wipes her bloody face with a handkerchief monogrammed with the name "Bill."[1] She says, "Bill, it's your baby," just before he shoots her.[2]

The next scene shows Beatrix arriving at a nice suburban home. Beatrix is there to kill Vernita Green, a former assassin turned housewife who, along with Bill, participated in the massacre at Beatrix's wedding rehearsal. As they are battling, Vernita's young daughter returns home from school. Vernita sends the girl to her room. The two women stop fighting and head to the kitchen for coffee. Beatrix tells Vernita she will not kill her in front of her daughter, and they agree to fight at another time. But then Vernita tries to shoot Beatrix, and Beatrix throws a knife at Vernita, killing her.

Waking Up

The action flashes back to the wedding chapel in El Paso, Texas, four years and six months earlier. The investigators at the chapel realize Beatrix is still alive. Next, Beatrix is seen lying in a hospital bed in a coma as a woman wearing an eye patch and disguised as a nurse prepares to inject her with a deadly drug. The woman is identified as Elle Driver, a member of the Deadly Viper Assassination Squad. Just as Elle is about to inject the poison, Bill calls to stop her, saying that killing Beatrix like that would "lower" them.

Four years later, Beatrix is lying in her hospital room when she suddenly awakens from her coma. Feeling her now-flat stomach, she cries out in anguish, "My baby!"[3] She hears someone coming and pretends to be still asleep. The man who enters the room is a hospital orderly named Buck, who has been selling access to her body while she is comatose. With him is a trucker, who pays $75 to rape Beatrix. Buck leaves, and as the trucker climbs on top of her, Beatrix attacks him. With the man now apparently dead on the floor, Beatrix climbs out of bed. Finding herself unable to walk, she crawls over to the prostrate man and takes a knife from him. When Buck returns, Beatrix kills him as well, taking his scrubs and the keys to his truck. She leaves the hospital in a wheelchair and finds the truck in the parking garage. Inside the truck, she concentrates on trying to revive movement in her feet and legs and thinks back on her assault four years earlier.

To Japan

The next segment tells the story of O-Ren Ishii, another member of the assassination squad. Done in Japanese-style animation, the sequence explains that at the age of 20, O-Ren is one of the top female assassins in the world. The animated segment ends and the action cuts back to Beatrix, who, after regaining control of her legs, drives off in the dead orderly's truck and flies to Okinawa, Japan.

Beatrix finds retired Japanese swordsmith and martial arts expert Hattori Hanzo on the Japanese island of Okinawa. Although he has vowed never again to make weapons, the swordsmith agrees to forge a weapon for Beatrix when she reveals that her intended victim is one of his former students— Bill.

The next scene shows O-Ren as a ruthless leader of all the Japanese gangster bosses. It then shows Beatrix in Tokyo. She follows O-Ren's lawyer, a woman named Sofie Fatale, to a restaurant where O-Ren is dining with her gangster army. Brief flashbacks indicate that both Sofie and O-Ren were

Beatrix Kiddo, *left*, and O-Ren Ishii fight at the end of *Kill Bill: Volume 1*.

present during the massacre at Beatrix's wedding rehearsal.

Beatrix calls out to O-Ren in Japanese, saying, "We have unfinished business!"[4] O-Ren sends her army of fighters to take on Beatrix, who defeats nearly all of them. Beatrix tells the survivors to leave, but she commands Sofie to stay. Beatrix and O-Ren duel with samurai swords. Beatrix wins, scalping O-Ren with her sword. She then dumps Sofie in a hospital parking lot, wishing to keep

Sofie alive to send a message to Bill that he will soon be dead, too. *Kill Bill: Volume 1* ends with an unseen Bill speaking to Sofie, asking her whether Beatrix knows her daughter is still alive.

The Massacre

Kill Bill: Volume 2 opens with the same scene that begins *Volume 1*. The Bride is lying on the floor, listening to Bill saying, "This is me at my most masochistic," before he shoots her.[5] Then, a scene shows Beatrix driving a car and vowing she is going to kill Bill.

The next scene shows Beatrix, visibly pregnant and wearing her white wedding dress, ready to marry a man named Tommy. Bill shows up during the rehearsal, and a surprised Beatrix introduces him as her father. As the rehearsal continues, four other members of the Deadly Viper Assassination Squad arrive, dressed in black. The massacre starts.

The next scene shows a trailer home in a barren desert landscape. Bill is there to warn his brother Budd that Beatrix is coming after them. Budd, who has retired from fighting, tells Bill he cannot dodge guilt. "That woman deserves her revenge," he says.[6]

Budd and Elle

In the next segment, Budd returns home to his trailer after being fired from his job. Beatrix, who has been crouched underneath the trailer, bursts in. Budd shoots her in the chest with a gun that shoots rock salt and injects her with a drug to knock her out. He calls Elle Driver, offering to sell her Beatrix's sword for $1 million. She agrees. Beatrix awakens and realizes she is tied up. Budd and an accomplice put her in a wooden coffin and bury her alive.

In the coffin, Beatrix recalls her training by Pai Mei, a legendary Chinese martial arts expert. Pai Mei was a master of the Five Point Palm Exploding Heart Technique, "the deadliest blow of all martial arts"—a technique so secret he had never even taught it to Bill.[7] He tried to teach Beatrix how to break a board just inches away from her body, but she was not successful in mastering the skill. Now, however, Beatrix unties herself and, with cold determination, breaks a hole in the coffin with her fist. She climbs up through the dirt and out of her grave.

In the next scene, Elle drives to Budd's trailer and pays him for Beatrix's sword. As Budd counts the money, a snake that was buried in the cash lashes out and strikes him. The snake is a black mamba— also Beatrix's code name—and its deadly venom quickly kills Budd. Elle calls Bill and lies that Beatrix has killed Budd. She starts to leave the trailer, but Beatrix arrives and the two fight viciously. Beatrix plucks out Elle's one remaining eye. Beatrix leaves carrying her sword, as Elle thrashes around blind in the trashed trailer with the deadly snake.

Revenge

In the final chapter of the saga, Beatrix tracks Bill to his home, arriving with her gun drawn and her sword across her back. She is stunned to encounter her daughter, B.B., who is pointing a toy gun at her and calling her "Mommy."[8] Bill explains that he told B.B. her mother was sleeping and would wake up some day. That evening, after B.B. is in bed, Bill shoots Beatrix with a dart filled with a truth serum and asks Beatrix why she left. She explains that she had to give up being an assassin once she learned she was going to be a mother.

Their discussion turns to Bill's attempt to kill her, and Beatrix admits she is still seeking revenge.

They start to fight using swords while sitting in Bill's backyard. Bill disarms her, but in a quick move, Beatrix reaches over and hits him five times in the chest. In that instant, a shocked Bill realizes that Pai Mei taught Beatrix the deadly Five Point Palm Exploding Heart Technique. He stands up, walks five steps, and dies. Beatrix leaves with her daughter and her sword. The movie ends with Beatrix and B.B. watching television cartoons together.

Beatrix arrives at Bill's house with her gun drawn.

Tarantino helped Uma Thurman with her role as Beatrix Kiddo.

10

How to Apply Feminist Criticism to *Kill Bill: Volume 1* and *Kill Bill: Volume 2*

What Is Feminist Criticism?

Feminist criticism considers an artistic work from the point of view of feminism, that is, the belief that women's opportunities and rights should be equal to those of men. Feminist critics often look at how women are portrayed in a book, film, or other works of art and evaluate whether common gender stereotypes are perpetuated by the work.

When completing a feminist critique of a movie, one might ask questions such as: Are women presented as equal to the male characters in the film? What kind of power do the female characters have? Where does their power come from? Some films may reassert common stereotypes of women as caretakers, objects of beauty, or partners who bow to the authority of men. Other films may subvert these traditional gender norms and present women as powerful and equal partners in their relationships with men. Applying feminist criticism can help you identify socially constructed ideas of femininity as they are reflected in a work.

Applying Feminist Criticism to *Kill Bill: Volume 1* and *Kill Bill: Volume 2*

The female characters in *Kill Bill: Volume 1* and *Kill Bill: Volume 2* defy traditional gender stereotypes. Far from damsels in distress, these women are assassins, martial arts experts, and gang leaders. They are physically and mentally strong enough to defeat the most vicious male opponents. Even once they become mothers, these women continue to be powerful adversaries, contradicting the common stereotype that women must choose between a career and motherhood. In fact, heroine Beatrix Kiddo is only able to fulfill her role as a mother once she embraces her ruthless and independent spirit. Through the story of Beatrix, the *Kill Bill* films assert that women can have power and be mothers.

Thesis Statement

The thesis statement is presented in the first paragraph: "Through the story of Beatrix, the *Kill Bill* films assert that women can have power and be mothers." This thesis addresses the question of how the *Kill Bill* films address women's roles as both career women and mothers.

At the beginning of the movie, Beatrix is about to get married and have a child, leaving behind her career as an assassin for a more conventional, domesticated life. Beatrix reaches this decision when, moments after discovering she is pregnant, she is surprised by a would-be assassin. She begs the assassin to spare her life for the sake of her unborn child. Beatrix decides that quitting her job is necessary to be a good mother. Soon after this decision, however, Beatrix is attacked and left for dead by Bill, her boss and former lover, who is angry that she left his assassination squad. Beatrix

Beatrix Kiddo is an expert swordswoman.

Argument One

The author has started to argue the thesis. This is the first argument: "Ironically, while Beatrix attempts to protect her child by adopting a more domesticated life, she actually puts her child in more danger by abandoning her career."

Argument Two

The author continues to argue the thesis by focusing on aspects of Beatrix's personality that make her a powerful assassin and, ultimately, a good mother: "In her quest to seek revenge, Beatrix proves her strength, independence, and determination."

is visibly pregnant and even tells Bill that she is carrying his baby, but this does not deter Bill. Ironically, while Beatrix attempts to protect her child by adopting a more domesticated life, she actually puts her child in more danger by abandoning her career.

In her quest to seek revenge, Beatrix proves her strength, independence, and determination. Beatrix is a well-trained assassin. She is an expert martial artist and swordswoman. Beatrix faces down the toughest of assailants and continually succeeds. Even when physically incapacitated in the hospital following a four-year-long coma, she is stronger than her opponents, speedily killing two villainous male rapists. Beatrix works independently, her only aid a sword received from Hattori Hanzo, and yet she is able to defeat an army of Japanese gangsters. Her determination to achieve revenge is emphasized to an almost ridiculous degree. Beatrix even breaks

At the end of the second film, Beatrix's strength and intelligence allow her to kill Bill, *left*, and reunite with her daughter.

her way out of a coffin and digs up through the dirt to escape.

It is only by returning to her former profession that Beatrix is able to recover her daughter and take on the role of motherhood. Beatrix returns to her life as an assassin when she begins tracking down the people on her "Death List." At the end of the second film, Beatrix finally tracks down Bill, who has been caring for their four-year-old daughter. Her path of revenge and brutality has led her to her daughter and given her the opportunity to become a mother.

> **Argument Three**
> The author next argues that Beatrix's power as an assassin allows her to become a mother: "It is only by returning to her former profession that Beatrix is able to recover her daughter and take on the role of motherhood."

When Beatrix meets her daughter for the first time, we see another part of her personality. Beatrix arrives at Bill's home with a gun drawn and a sword slung on her back only to be disarmed by her daughter pointing a toy gun at her and calling her "Mommy."[1] She watches television with her daughter and tucks her into bed. <u>The ruthlessness of an assassin and the nurturing instinct of a mother coexist in Beatrix's personality. She can be both powerful and motherly.</u>

Soon after, Beatrix confronts and kills Bill. It is because of her strength and intelligence in mastering the Five Point Palm Exploding Heart Technique that she is finally able to kill Bill and "rescue" her daughter from him. Beatrix leaves Bill's house with her daughter *and* her sword, further suggesting that although they have to struggle to do so, women can retain their worldly power even as they take on the role of motherhood.

Argument Four

Here, the author expands on the point that Beatrix can be a mother and retain her power: "The ruthlessness of an assassin and the nurturing instinct of a mother coexist in Beatrix's personality. She can be both powerful and motherly."

Conclusion

This final paragraph is the conclusion of the critique. It sums up the author's arguments and partially restates the original thesis, which has now been argued and supported with evidence.

Thinking Critically about *Kill Bill: Volume 1* and *Kill Bill: Volume 2*

Now it is your turn to assess the critique. Consider these questions:

1. The thesis claims that the *Kill Bill* movies promote women as mothers and individuals with social power. Do you agree? Why or why not?

2. This critique focuses on the main character Beatrix Kiddo. Do you think the thesis could be applied to other female characters in the film? If so, how? What other roles do female characters have in the film?

3. What arguments in the critique were the most convincing? Which were least convincing? Why?

Other Approaches

What you have just read is one possible way to apply feminist criticism to *Kill Bill: Volume 1* and *Kill Bill: Volume 2*. Recall that feminist criticism examines a work to determine how it reflects women and their roles in society. Following are two alternate approaches.

Kill Bill as Empowering to Women

The *Kill Bill* movies may be seen as empowering to women, as the female victims in the films become powerful avengers. For example, Beatrix fights back against the men who raped her while she was comatose, and then hunts down the people who attacked her and killed her family. O-Ren Ishii also wreaks a bloody revenge on the man who killed her parents and later attempted to rape her. Overall, the film sends a message that violence against women, sexual and otherwise, is not to be tolerated.

The thesis statement for such a critique might be: The *Kill Bill* films denounce violence against women by showing that those who commit violent acts against women are severely punished.

Kill Bill as Violent Entertainment

Some critics have asserted that violent female characters in the film do not make much of a statement for female power. Instead, they argue, the film simply provides entertaining fight scenes. Critic Emma Young is one who questions common feminist interpretations of the film, writing: "Women killing women in a hysterically violent manner for the satisfaction of a largely male audience is girl power?"[2]

The thesis statement for such a critique could be: The *Kill Bill* films do not serve as feminist films that empower women, but, rather, provide violent entertainment aimed at a male audience.

You Critique It

Now that you have learned about several different critical theories and how to apply them to film, are you ready to perform a critique of your own? You have read that this type of evaluation can help you look at film from a new perspective and make you pay attention to issues you may not have otherwise recognized. So, why not use one of the critical theories profiled in this book to consider a fresh take on your favorite movie?

First, choose a theory and the movie you want to analyze. Remember that the theory is a springboard for asking questions about the work.

Next, write a specific question that relates to the theory you have selected. Then you can form your thesis, which should provide the answer to that question. Your thesis is the most important part of your critique and offers an argument about the work based on the tenets, or beliefs, of the theory you are applying. Recall that the thesis statement typically appears at the very end of the introductory paragraph of your essay. It is usually only one sentence long.

After you have written your thesis, find evidence to back it up. Good places to start are in the work itself or journals or articles that discuss what other people have said about it. Since you are critiquing a movie, you may also want to read about the screenwriter's life to get a sense of what factors may have affected the creative process. This can be especially useful if working within historical or auteur criticism.

Depending on which theory you apply, you can often find evidence in the film's dialogue, plot, setting, or soundtrack. You should also explore parts of the movie that seem to disprove your thesis and create an argument against them. As you do this, you might want to address what other critics have written about the movie. Their quotes may help support your claim.

Before you start analyzing a work, think about the different arguments made in this book. Reflect on how evidence supporting the thesis was presented. Did you find that some of the techniques used to back up the arguments were more convincing than others? Try these methods as you prove your thesis in your own critique.

When you are finished writing your critique, read it over carefully. Is your thesis statement understandable? Do the supporting arguments flow logically, with the topic of each paragraph clearly stated? Can you add any information that would present your readers with a stronger argument in favor of your thesis? Were you able to use quotes from the movie, as well as from other critics, to enhance your ideas?

Did you see the work in a new light?

Timeline

1963 Quentin Tarantino is born in Knoxville, Tennessee, on March 27.

1997 Tarantino releases *Jackie Brown*, which he directed and wrote based on Elmore Leonard's book *Rum Punch*.

2009 *Inglourious Basterds* is released.

2003 *Kill Bill: Volume 1* is released.

2004 *Kill Bill: Volume 2* is released.

2005 Tarantino directs episodes of the television show *CSI*.

2007 *Death Proof* is released as part of the double feature *Grindhouse*.

1983 Tarantino starts working as a clerk at Video Archives.

1987 Tarantino shows his first film, *My Best Friend's Birthday,* written with acting class friend Craig Hamann.

1988 Tarantino appears on the television series *The Golden Girls* on November 19.

1992 *Reservoir Dogs* debuts at the Sundance Film Festival on January 18.

1994 *Pulp Fiction* is released.

Pulp Fiction wins the Palme d'Or, the highest prize at the Cannes Film Festival.

Natural Born Killers, based on a story by Tarantino, comes out.

1995 *Pulp Fiction* wins an Academy Award and a Golden Globe for best screenplay.

Tarantino guest-directs an episode of the television show *ER,* which airs on May 11.

Four Rooms, written and codirected by Tarantino, comes to theatres.

Glossary

analyze
> To examine in detail.

assert
> To state with certainty.

bail
> Money or bond paid to the court system by a person charged with a crime in order to obtain release from jail while awaiting trial.

bail bondsman
> A person who, for a fee, pledges money on behalf of a person charged with a crime.

blaxploitation
> A film genre of the 1970s which featured African-American actors and often presented stereotyped African-American characters.

cinematic
> Relating to movies.

collaboration
> A project or task done by two or more people working together.

contradict
> To state an opposing point of view.

film noir
> A type of movie that is fatalistic and cynical and generally centers around crime or corruption.

homoerotic
> Concerning sexual desire between people of the same sex.

juxtaposition

A side-by-side placement of objects or ideas.

linear narrative

A story that starts at a point in time and ends at a later point in time.

moral

Relating to the distinctions between right and wrong.

narrative

A story told in chronological order.

nostalgia

A longing and appreciation for a happy period of time in the past.

perspective

A point of view.

Bibliography of Works and Criticism

Important Works

Reservoir Dogs (1992)

True Romance (1993)

Pulp Fiction (1994)

Natural Born Killers (1994)

Four Rooms (1995)

From Dusk Till Dawn (1996)

Jackie Brown (1997)

Kill Bill: Volume 1 (2003)

Kill Bill: Volume 2 (2004)

Sin City (2005)

Death Proof (2007)

Inglourious Basterds (2009)

Critical Discussions

Bourzereau, Laurent. *Ultraviolent Movies: From Sam Peckinpah to Quentin Tarantino*. Secaucus, NJ: Carol Publishing Group, 1996.

Davis, Todd F., and Kenneth Womack. "Shepherding the Weak: The Ethics of Redemption in Quentin Tarantino's *Pulp Fiction*." *Literature/Film Quarterly*. 1988: 60–66.

Indiana, Gary, and Bell Hooks, Jeanne Silverthorne, Dennis Cooper, Robert Paul Wood. "Pulp the hype on the Q.T." *Artforum International*. Mar. 1995.

Irwin, Mark. "Pulp & the Pulpit: The Films of Quentin Tarantino and Robert Rodriquez." *Literature and Theology*. 12.1 (1998): 70-81.

Resources

Selected Bibliography

Charyn, Jerome. *Raised by Wolves: The Turbulent Art and Times of Quentin Tarantino*. New York: Thunder's Mouth, 2006.

Dawson, Jeff. *Quentin Tarantino: The Cinema of Cool*. New York: Applause Books, 1995.

Gallafent, Edward. *Quentin Tarantino*. Harlow, England: Pearson Education, 2006.

Woods, Paul A. *King Pulp: The Wild World of Quentin Tarantino*. New York: Thunder's Mouth, 2006.

Further Reading

Hamilton, John. *Screenplay*. Mankato, MN: Abdo & Daughters, 2009.

Lommel, Cookie. *African Americans in Film and Television*. Philadelphia, PA: Chelsea House Publishers, 2003.

Miles, Liz. *Writing a Screenplay*. Chicago, IL: Heinemann-Raintree, 2010.

Platt, Richard. *Eyewitness: Film*. New York: Dorling Kindersley, 2000.

Web Links

To learn more about critiquing the works of Quentin
Tarantino, visit ABDO Publishing Company online at
www.abdopublishing.com. Web sites about the works
of Quentin Tarantino are featured on our Book Links
page. These links are routinely monitored and updated to
provide the most current information available.

For More Information

Museum of the Moving Image
3601 35th Avenue, Long Island City, NY 11106
718-784-4520
www.movingimage.us

The Museum of the Moving Image houses artifacts of
the film industry. It also holds film screenings.

San Francisco Film Museum
1755 Van Ness Avenue, Suite 101, San Francisco, CA
94109
415-652-0249
sanfranciscofilmmuseum.org

The San Francisco Film Museum examines the history
of filmmaking.

Source Notes

Chapter 1. Introduction to Critiques

None.

Chapter 2. A Closer Look at Quentin Tarantino

1. Jeff Dawson. *Quentin Tarantino: The Cinema of Cool.*
New York: Applause Books, 1995. 22.

2. Vincent Canby. "Review/Film: A Caper Goes Wrong,
Resoundingly." *New York Times*. 23 Oct. 1992. 20 Mar. 2010
<http://www.nytimes.com/1992/10/23/movies/review-film-a-
caper-goeswrong-resoundingly.html?pagewanted=1>.

3. Tim Appelo. "Quentin Tarantino." *Entertainment
Weekly*. 30 Dec. 1994.

Chapter 3. An Overview of *Reservoir Dogs*

1. *Reservoir Dogs*. Dir. Quentin Tarantino. Miramax
Films, 1992.

2. Ibid.

3. Ibid.

4. Ibid.

5. Ibid.

**Chapter 4. How to Apply Gender Criticism to *Reservoir
Dogs***

1. Jeff Dawson. *Quentin Tarantino: The Cinema of Cool.*
New York: Applause Books, 1995. 74.

2. Gary Indiana, Bell Hooks, Jeanne Silverthorne, Dennis
Cooper, and Robert Paul Wood. "Pulp the hype on the Q.T."
Artforum International. Mar. 1995.

Chapter 5. An Overview of *Pulp Fiction*

    1. *Pulp Fiction*. Dir. Quentin Tarantino. Miramax Films, 1994.

    2. Ibid.

    3. Ibid.

Chapter 6. How to Apply New Criticism to *Pulp Fiction*

    1. *Pulp Fiction*. Dir. Quentin Tarantino. Miramax Films, 1994.

    2. Ibid.

    3. Ibid.

    4. Todd F. Davis and Kenneth Womack. "Shepherding the Weak: The Ethics of Redemption in Quentin Tarantino's Pulp Fiction." *Literature/Film Quarterly*. 1988: 65.

Chapter 7. An Overview of *Jackie Brown*

    1. *Jackie Brown*. Dir. Quentin Tarantino. Miramax Films, 1997.

    2. Ibid.

Chapter 8. How to Apply Historical Criticism to *Jackie Brown*

    1. *Jackie Brown*. Dir. Quentin Tarantino. Miramax Films, 1997.

    2. Ibid.

    3. Ibid.

    4. Ibid.

    5. Ibid.

Source Notes Continued

Chapter 9. An Overview of *Kill Bill: Volume 1* and *Kill Bill: Volume 2*

1. *Kill Bill: Volume 1*. Dir. Quentin Tarantino. Miramax Films, 2003.

2. Ibid.

3. Ibid.

4. Ibid.

5. *Kill Bill: Volume 2*. Dir. Quentin Tarantino. Miramax Films, 2004.

6. Ibid.

7. Ibid.

8. Ibid.

Chapter 10. How to Apply Feminist Criticism to *Kill Bill: Volume 1* and *Kill Bill: Volume 2*

1. *Kill Bill: Volume 2*. Dir. Quentin Tarantino. Miramax Films, 2004.

2. Emma Young. "Sticks and Stones May Break Bones But Not Stereotypes." *The Sydney Morning Herald*. 27 Oct. 2003. 22 Feb. 2010 <http:// www.smh.com.au/ articles/2003/10/26/1067103267287.html?from=storyrhs>.

Index

Index

About the Author

Mary K. Pratt is a freelance journalist based in Massachusetts. She writes for a variety of publications, including newspapers, magazines, and trade journals. She has covered topics ranging from business to fashion.

Photo Credits

Franco Origlia/Getty Images, cover, 3; Armando Gallo/Retna Ltd./Corbis, 12; CORBIS SYGMA, 15; Joel Ryan/AP Images, 17, 98; Live Entertainment/Photofest, 25, 26, 31; Miramax Films/Photofest, 18, 29, 36, 39, 44, 51, 56, 61, 63, 64, 66, 71, 76, 81, 85, 86, 89, 91, 99; Buena Vista Pictures/Photofest, 41, 46